CAT
POEMS

Also by Jacintha Buddicom

The Compleat Works of Cini Willoughby Dering
The Happy Hedgehogs
The Young Eric (In *The World of George Orwell*)

CAT POEMS

by

JACINTHA BUDDICOM

Illustrated by the Author

LESLIE FREWIN of LONDON

First published in 1973 by
Leslie Frewin Publishers Limited,
Five Goodwin's Court,
Saint Martin's Lane,
London WC2N 4LL, England.

Set in Univers Medium,
Printed at The Compton Press Ltd.,
Compton Chamberlayne,
Salisbury, Wiltshire,
England.

ISBN 0 85632 066 8

THIS LITTLE BOOK IS DEDICATED

To my sister GUINEVER
who kindly tolerates my cats,

To ALEXANDER CATULLUS and
ROBERTSON CATT, ESQUIRE
who share the lion's share of hearth and home,

And from long ago and far away,
between the lines and through the pages,
the remembrance of THE OTHERS.

Introduction

These cat songs, which nearly all have tunes, are not in the order in which they were written, but arranged more logically so that one follows on another. They are of various kinds: some are short, some long; some traditional, some modern; some rhyme, some don't. There are some to suit all ages, from a nursery-rhyme finger-game for babies of two *Five Little Kittens* to a music-hall song for great-grandpa, *Pretty Mrs. Pussycat*. The sentimental might like *A Golden Cat Song*, the sophisticated *Lament for a Literary Lady*, and the philosophical *Reincarnation*, or *Relativity*, or *Undriven Snow*.

Some are frivolous, some are sad. There seems to be rather a prevalence of Remembrances for Departed Cats, but their lives – all nine of them – are often of brief duration, and these elegies might be of comfort to someone who has lost a cat. No cat can ever be replaced: but a good home should not be left abandoned when it could be a refuge for some pitiful creature in need of care and shelter. There are three on this theme: *A Cat is a King, Phoenix*, and *New Cat*, besides the requiem for *Albuericus Pawpins Beadle*.

There are four of remembered moments: *The Tabbycat in the Shropshire Barn* was a very long time ago, but the beauty of her kittens chasing those clouds of blue butterflies in their sunny cornfield will never be forgotten. And *Quillie*, the first cat I ever had, when I was a child, is even further back in the past: we loved each other dearly. She was a very little cat, of great intelligence, and she had many families of prize-winning kittens for whom there was a long waiting-list of fervent would-be homes. For them no such fate as might befall the *Four White Kittens*. But *Quillie* herself disappeared: when I came home one half-term from boarding-school she was not there. We never discovered what became of her: she was a great huntress and very beautiful. *Two Solstices* is for her, and for Rod McKuen's lost cat *Sloopy*.

Searching in a Dark Room is pure description of cat, and so are the *Transports of an Anti-Travelling Kitten*. One is social history *Luck of the Draw*, and one natural history *Feline Fact*. Two might be classed as impartial inventories, *Names and More Names*, and one as phonetic *The Poet Deprecates English Orthography*. Two Prime Ministers cats are recorded – of opposing parties, *Churchill and Jock*, and *Nemo's Song*.

Two are sheer nonsenses: *A Christmas Song for Lollipop* and *Politicat*. There are two operettas: *Lollipop's Birthday* and *Cor Leonis*. (*Cor Leonis* is really rather an alien stranger . . . it properly belongs to the Kabala lot, but there *IS* a cat in it, so it is included in the cat category.)

Tryst was written after a visit to our old home at Shiplake many years later. Alexander Catullus, my white Lollipop-Lexey, stayed there too. I found him on the lawn in the very early morning, darting and dancing as though he had an invisible companion. So *Tryst* joins the first and last cats together, and perhaps dear old *Christopher* was playing with them too.

Finally, there is the *Kittens Carol*, from the legend of the kitten with the Virgin and Christchild in the stable at Bethlehem: Lexey's offering to all kittens everywhere, and mine to all who love cats.

Bognor Regis, 1973   Jacintha Buddicom

Contents

LUCK OF THE DRAW

If I had lived four thousand years ago
In Egypt:
Because I like cats
I should have lived
To be
High Priestess to the great Cat-Goddess Bast,
Protectress of the Pharaoh's granaries.

If I had lived four hundred years ago
In Europe:
Treating my little cat with simple kindness
Because I like cats,
I should have lived
To be
Bound to a stake be-ringed by leaping flames,
Burned as a witch for my illicit love.

Fortune ordained that I should live today
In England
To go my way in peace:
Neither revered with homage
Nor condemned to torture
Because I like cats.

BLUE PERSIAN
Portrait of QUILLIE *as a Young Cat*

Long dark grey fur
And Egypt in your eyes
Your Nile-green eyes
My kitten Cleopatra:
What Lion-mouse
Will fall beneath your paws
Your soft swift paws
My innocent Bubastis?

What Caesar sleeps
Surrendered to your guile
As you beguile
The Sun beyond the solstice?
Where sun meets moon
And night and day are one
All one to you
Enigma of all Sphinxes.

The Cat is a nocturnal animal.

TWO SOLSTICES
For Rod McKuen

I was a pigtailed schoolgirl
at boarding-school in Oxford.
When I came home
for the half-term holiday
Quillie was gone.

He was a young writer
living in a New York flat.
When he came home
from a night and a day away
Sloopy was gone.

    He searched the concrete canyons of the streets
        Through drifts of town-grey Christmas snow in vain:
    As I – past miles and years our bondage meets –
        Searched every green Midsummer English lane.

My heart turns over for him
and my hand
reaches to touch his own
in silent comfort.

How many lesser deaths we die ourselves
not knowing
what befell them
remembering
how they loved us:

                My lost Blue Persian
                lost so long ago
                gone hunting once too often
                in the fields,
                and his little American cat
                no longer safe
                on her city windowcill
                among the avocados.

15

SEARCHING IN A DARK ROOM FOR A BLACK CAT THAT ISN'T THERE

A cat is a leaf in the wind —
His eyes twin stars in a midnight sky —
Illusive, intangible, swift
As a May-day dragonfly:
His love is his royal gift —
Nor fear nor favour his favour buy —
That Self he will never rescind:
That primal, ultimate *I AM I*.

Conversation Piece:

Unsolicited Critic: Don't you mean EL-usive?

Jacintha: No I don't. If I had, I would have said so. EL-usive is just something you can't catch hold of. ILL-usive is not only something you can't catch hold of, you're not even sure if it's really there.

Unsolicited Critic: And all these mixed metaphors – leaves in the wind –
(Soldiering on) Mayday dragonflies – midnight stars. . . .

Jacintha: Aren't they gorgeous? Just like cats.
(unabashed) I thought of sub-titling it:
    'Mr. Speaker I smell a rat. . . .
    Here be similes for a CAT.'

    'Mister Speaker I smell a rat,
    I see him floating in the air,
    But I will nip
    Him in the bud. . . .
    For if you look to see a cat
    You find it is no longer there –
    We all knew THAT
    In Noah's ship
    Before the flood.'

Unsolicited Critic: Oh, all right, all right. You needn't go ON. Let's get
(Very tetchily) back to what's in the BOOK, and see what's wrong with the NEXT one.

THE POET DEPRECATES ENGLISH ORTHOGRAPHY

That
Rhymes with CAT:
But *what*
Does NOT.

The Unsolicited Critic, *making a great parade of counting loudly on his fingers that there are 35 letters in the Title and only 31 in the Verse, merely sulks 'I don't call eight words a POEM', and forbears further comment.*

Two Poems About A
TABBYCAT WITH YOUNG KITTENS IN AN ANCIENT BARN

I :
Safe in their citadel of soft dry hay
They dream the night away :
Then sleep again. Long after
They wake with mewing laughter
When the noon sun, sky-high, winks at them through every roofless
   rafter.

II.
They lived in an old grey timbered barn
In Shropshire,
Beside a cornfield
Alight with blue butterflies.
The kittens chased the butterflies
In the evening sun :
They could not catch them.
Their mother did not bother with butterflies
She was more interested
In a nest of fieldmice –
Butterflies are beautiful
But fieldmice or young leverets
Make a more substantial supper.

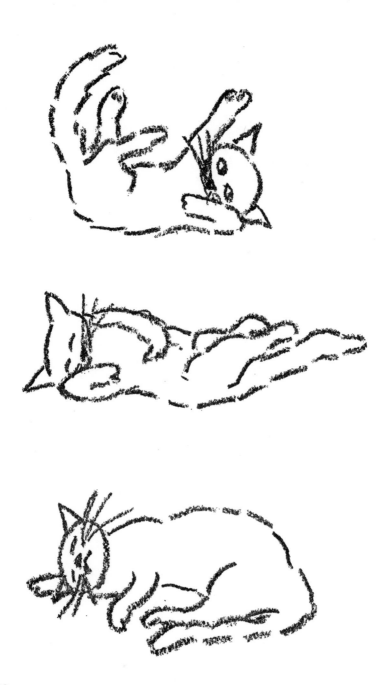

A CAT IS A KING

A cat is a king:
When the king is dead long live the king . . . and so
Out of the terror, the torrent, the tempest, the snow,
Under the wing
Of that king
Who was once at our fireside and now
Is gone with the blossom that drifted in Spring
From the bough,
Some pitiful waif
When it hears
The murmuring token that ends all the hungers and fears
Shall come from the darkness and danger at last to be safe.

For the old cat, kind ghost,
Guides the new kittens path
Leading it home through the storm:
So the ones he loved most
Keep his place by the hearth
And his memory warm.

*If any Cat Lover, by remote mischance, has not yet come
across Monty's Book* A Cat in the Window, *and Lama's Book*
LAMA . . . *and the other books in which they are mentioned
by Derek Tangye, there is a delicious* Treat in Store.

PHOENIX

The big brave Angel Cat, folding a rainbow wing,
Stretched out his gentle paw
From Cat-Elysium's door:
I'll find,
Purred he,
A kitten . . . you were kind,
You must not grieve for me . . .
A kitten's comforting.

This one might do, this little timid stray
Terrestrial night to my celestial day:
It cannot take my place,
No other could do that,
But though you cannot bring me back
You might retrace
Remembrance in a kitten's pansy-face.

I, your lost lion cat, am now at one
With the eternal saffron-tawney sun:
But still your heart some tenderness may hold
For kitten white or black
As well as cat
Of gold
Who once grew old.

The big brave Angel Cat, shaking his feathery mane,
Drew back a languid paw
From Cat-Elysium's door:
Turned round
And bowed
Three times without a sound . . .
Then curled up on his cloud
And went to sleep again.

Another song for Monty and Lama, also in remembrance of Boy-Boy, *my beautiful cream Persian* Raphaelito Fox, *another golden cat: who was run over and killed before he was four years old. His chosen companion was little* Alexander Catullus, *the white kitten* Lollipop.

LOLLIPOP'S BIRTHDAY
Song for small children

Scene: A market with stalls, including a hat stall, a toy stall, and a fish stall.

Enter CHILDREN, counting their money and singing:

Chorus: It's his birthday tomorrow: so we're going out to shop
          To buy a birthday present: for the White Cat Lollipop.

All: What shall we buy for the Little White Cat?
*Girl: Shall we buy him a HAT?
Boys: No, he wouldn't like THAT!
Girls: Not a beautiful HAT
          For a little cat's HEAD
          With a bobble of BLUE
          And a ribbon-rose of RED?
All   That wouldn't DO
but *:   For our QUAD-RU-PED.
          No, he wouldn't like THAT
          So, we won't buy a HAT. . . .
All: WHAT shall we buy for the Little White Cat?

All: What shall we buy for the Little White Cat?
*Boy: Shall we buy him a BAT?
Girls: No, he wouldn't like THAT!
Boys: Not a beautiful BAT
          For a little cat's PAW
          Made of willow brand-NEW
          Like he never saw beFORE?
All   That wouldn't DO
but *:   For our CON-QUER-OR.
          No, he wouldn't like THAT
          So, we won't buy a BAT. . . .
All: WHAT shall we buy for the Little White Cat?

All:	What shall we buy for the Little White Cat?
Baby:	Shall we buy him a SPRAT?
All:	Yes, he's SURE to like THAT!
Girls:	Yes, a salmon or SPRAT
Boys:	For a little cat's TUM
Girls:	And a tin of pilchards TOO
Boys:	For a Piscatory PLUM.
All:	THAT ought to DO
	For our PAN-JAM-DRUM.
	Yes, he's SURE to like THAT
	Pilchard, salmon and SPRAT. . . .
	We shall buy FISH for the Little White Cat:
	FISH
	Is the DISH
	He would WISH. . . .
	We all know THAT!
	So WE shall buy FISH for the Little White Cat.
Envoy:	It's his birthday tomorrow: so we're going out to shop
	To buy a birthday present: for the White Cat Lollipop.

All crowd round the fish stall, buying fish. The biggest boy walks off holding up a sprat between his finger and thumb; the smallest child ('BABY') drags an enormous salmon by the tail; and the others wave tins of pilchards, as the Curtain falls.

His name is really Alexander Catullus (Alley-Cat *dolled up) because he had a Siamese grandfather, though the rest of him is more or less white Persian: but as he is deaf, you can call him pretty well anything. When he is GOOD (always . . . well, almost always) he is my Lollipop Boy. When he is BAD (never . . . well, not awfully often) he is my Polliwog Boy. And at Christmas Time he is my Hollyberry Boy, as part of the Christmas decoration: he is very decorative. So here is –*

A CHRISTMAS SONG FOR LOLLIPOP

Jacintha : Oh Christmas comes
And Christmas goes
 With Christmas plums
And a Christmas rose
And the rest
Of the jolly
Merry
Joy –
But the best
Is my Holly
Berry
Boy.

The Old Year ends
And the New Year starts
 With faithful friends
And strange sweet-hearts
Through East-
er and Whits-
un and Michael-
muss
The best beast
Of all kits
Is my lickle
Puss.

Lollipop : This baby-chat
Is undignified
I am a cat
And a cat has pride
Which you shock —
Dry, restrictionary
Dust,
Old Stodge,
THE DOC
Wrote his dictionary
Just
For HODGE.

Jacintha : Well, THIS Christmas goes
And NEXT Christmas will come
With a white Christmas rose
And a black Christmas plum
But all the year through
Don't let
Folly
Decoy —
I'll be faithful to you
My pet
Lolli-
Pop Boy.

The white Christmas rose for Lollipop, and the black Christmas plum for Lama. Folly once almost decoyed when I went to the Cat Show and was sorely tempted by the beauty of two Cream Persian brothers, Boysie and Puffkin. . . . I picked them out BEFORE they were judged, and they BOTH won prizes. But I restrained myself, and have prudently avoided cat shows ever since.

Boswell on Dr. Johnson:
'I shall never forget the indulgence with which he treated his cat HODGE; for whom he himself used to go out and buy oysters lest the servants having that trouble should take a dislike to the poor creature. I recollect him one day scrambling up Dr. Johnson's breast, apparently with much satisfaction, while my friend smiling rubbed down his back and pulled him by the tail; and when I observed he was a fine cat, saying 'Why, yes, Sir, but I have had cats I liked better than this.' And then, as if perceiving Hodge to be out of countenance adding 'But he is a very fine cat, a very fine cat indeed.'

LOLLIPOP, however, may be slightly exaggerating when he asserts that the DICTIONARY was compiled entirely for Hodge's own benefit.

If you WANT Baby-Talk ('I DON'T', says Lollipop) here is a
NURSERY RHYME: or BABIES GAME:

FIVE LITTLE KITTENS

FIVE little kittens went out to play
    Dum dum diddledum
    Dum dum DAW
One thought he'd stray a bit further away
    Dum dum diddledum
    Then there were FOUR.

FOUR little kittens went out to shop
    Dum dum diddledum
    Dum dum DEE
One thought he'd stop to eat a lamb chop
    Dum dum diddledum
    Then there were THREE.

THREE little kittens went out to sing
    Dum dum diddledum
    Dum dum DOO
One silly thing his guitar forgot to bring
    Dum dum diddledum
    Then there were TWO.

TWO little kittens went out to dance
    Dum dum diddledum
    Dum dum DUN
One said they prance much better in France
    Dum dum diddledum
    Then there was ONE.

ONE little kitten went over to France
    Dum dum diddledum
    Dum dum DOO
He BROUGHT BACK HIS FRIEND for another dance
    Dum dum diddledum
    Then there were TWO.

TWO little kittens went out to sing
   Dum dum diddledum
   Dum dum DEE
A GUITAR FOR THEIR FRIEND they remembered to bring
   Dum dum diddledum
   Then there were THREE.

THREE little kittens went out to shop
   Dum dum diddledum
   Dum dum DAW
They BROUGHT BACK THEIR FRIEND who had finished his chop
   Dum dum diddledum
   Then there were FOUR.

FOUR little kittens went out to play
   Dum dum diddledum
   Dum dum DEN
They BROUGHT BACK THEIR FRIEND who'd strayed further away
   And then there were FIVE little kittens again.

This can start all over again and go on for ever.
For small babies, it makes a finger-game, hiding one finger at a time and
then bringing them one-by-one back again.
Older toddlers can play it representing the kittens themselves: it is best
played with five lined up and one more as compere. All sing the first
line, then the compere counts them out to DUM DUM DIDDLEDUM :
the one falling to DAW *must run off to one corner of the playspace as*
the STRAYAWAY *kitten. Similarly with the other verses, to the other*
corners till only one child is left. After singing as far as DOO *in the next*
verse, he fetches back the BETTER-IN-FRANCE *kitten from its corner,*
and similarly with the other verses till all are back again.
Fewer than five children can commandeer dolls, teddy-bears etc.: to
make up the number, but NOT *the family cats. Dogs, however, can be*
taught to play this game quite efficiently.

PRETTY MRS. PUSSYCAT
A Music-Hall song

Period: The late 1890's or early 1900's.
The Singer: A MAIDEN LADY, with pince-nez and knitting.
The Dancers: all with cat-masks and nylon-fur paw-gloves:
PRETTY MRS. PUSSYCAT, very fluffy and frilly.
THE GINGER TOM, with striped blazer and straw hat.
THE BIG BLACK BOSS, with city suit and bowler (or morning suit and topper).
THE TABBY, a respectable workman with cloth cap.
Chorus: Male and Female as available: Audience join in.

While the SINGER sings, and to the music between the verses, the DANCERS dance and mime: but they remain as a TABLEAU during the singing of the CHORUS, which is first sung by the chorus themselves, and then repeated by the audience.

I have a pretty pussycat: she made a pretty Bride
But her husband caught the cat-flu and very sadly died.
So Pretty Mrs. Pussycat sedately went to stay
For a little summer holiday at Bognor Regis Bay.
Pretty Mrs. Pussycat, strolling on the Prom,
Strolling on the Prom met a handsome Ginger Tom:
Pretty Mrs. Pussycat, choosing candy-floss,
Choosing candy-floss was chosen by the Big Black Boss:
Pretty Mrs. Pussycat, exploring Hotham Park,
Exploring Hotham Park a Tabby found her in the dark. . . .

Chorus: OOOOOOOOH !!!
WHAT a fine adventure for a Pretty Pussy Cat!!!
WHAT a fine adventure for a Pretty Pussy Cat!!!
(*Audience repeat Chorus*).

Soon Pretty Mrs. PUSSCAT to my Chelsea home came back
Accompanied by the GINGER – and the TABBY – and the BLACK.
'THREE husbands, Mrs. PUSSYCAT? That's really rather much !
They'll have to work to keep themselves – you've heard of Treating Dutch ?'

They settled down quite nicely: they all found things to do.
The Tabby got a job as jobbing gardener down at Kew,
The Ginger ran a fish-shop with a Special Bognor Range,
And the Big Black Boss made thousands on the Stock
    Exchange.

Chorus: OOOOOOOOH!!!
           WHAT a fine achievement for a Clever Pussy Cat!!!
           WHAT a fine achievement for a Clever Pussy Cat!!!

Last week inside my hat-box — I was going out to tea —
I found my Pretty Pussy Cat with kittens one — two — three —
    'Good Gracious Mrs. Pussycat! Now where did THEY
        come from?
    There's a BLACK ONE — and a TABBY — and a TINY
        GINGER TOM!'

The three males of the household all back from work that
    night
 Were overwhelmed with pleasure, with pride and with
    delight:
The TABBY brought a bunch of flowers, the GINGER fish &
    chips,
And the BIG BLACK BOSS champagne all round, to launch
    Their Kittenships.
But, purring to the kittens, I heard Pretty PUSSCAT say:
    'I MIGHT go back again next year to Bognor Regis Bay'

Chorus: OOOOOOOOH!!!
           ANOTHER nice Adventure for a Pretty Pussy Cat???
           ANOTHER nice Adventure for a Pretty Pussy Cat!!!

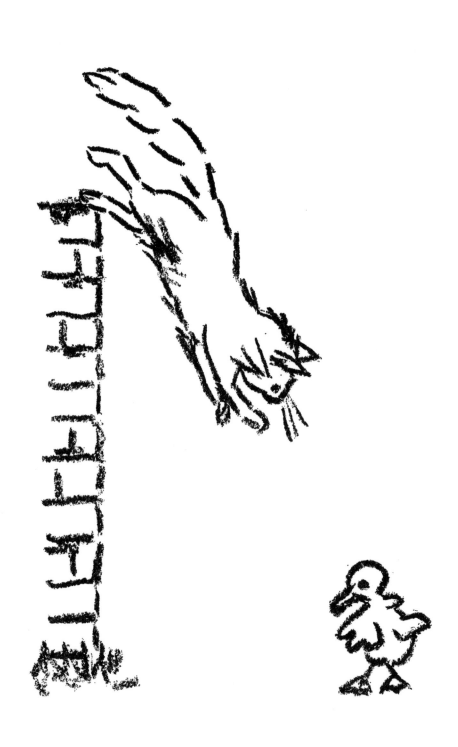

NAMES

Some names for cats are custom-made
They seem exactly right:
Like ROBERTSON my marmalade
Or LOLLIPOP my white.

My marmalade is ROBERTSON
Because I think it super:
Aunt Flossie had a ginger one
But he was christened COOPER.

CHRISTOPHER – bane of every dog –
His tales would fill a tome –
Once found my Uncle lost in fog
And led him safely home.

Brave RAFEY – RAPHAELITO FOX
So-called for Doctor Brooks –
A big Cream Persian laughed at locks
And captured rats and rooks.

Then pretty little TIDDY came,
 White short-haired, sweet and fat:
They said 'Oh what a silly name!' –
She was a silly cat.

*Of course, there's no such thing as a silly cat: some just
don't exhibit their intelligence quite so ostentatiously
as others. Tiddy could be very, very clever indeed when
it suited her. And Rafey could OPEN DOORS. He was a
great hunter, too: he caught a bus to Brighton once.*

MORE NAMES:

I: CARD INDEX
Katie and Pat
Had a cat
Whom they christened
Quite cleverly
PICKLES:
A nomenclature not bad
But which lots of other kittens have already had.
Pat and Kate
Demonstrate
They might better have listened
To Beverley
Nichols
Whose feline family happily thrive
Addressed as ONE . . . and FOUR . . . and FIVE.

Though this may seem Indolence's inert
Somnolescent
Ember
A-slumber,
Rather than Imagination's alert
Iridescent
Awakening flame,
It's considerably harder to remember
The proper NUMBER
Than an infinitely easier, effervescent,
Extrovert
NAME.

MORE NAMES:

II: TRANSPORTS OF AN ANTI-TRAVELLING
KITTEN

My Boss brought me home in his Boss-Car –
To motors I'm not reconciled –
While he crooned Traviata and Tosca
Till I spat at him, even more riled –
So he said he would call me OSCAR
Because
I was
So wild.

III: REINCARNATION

Some merit special habitats:
Thus Hugo Wolf is two separate cats,
But a certain poet, with verse too free,
Is only the left hind leg of a flea.
Poor flea, I pray
Wherever YOU go,
You'll keep away
From WOLF and HUGO.

*These, of course, are Beverley Nichols' cats, so charm-
ing on the Cat Calendar . . . and elsewhere. And so too
was the remarkable OSCAR.*

RELATIVITY

Mice,
Said the Cat, are nice :
I've tasted them once or twice.
May the Great Cat Sun
Ere my ninth life's done
Ponder this good advice :

That a Heavenly house
Without a mouse,
Or a Heavenly flat
Without a rat,
Or a Heavenly view
Without a shrew,
Or the Heavenly Whole
Without a vole
or a mole

Wouldn't be Paradise.

Undoubtedly Many Mansions would include a
Home for the Hunter, agreed Quillie, and Leo, and
Rafey, and little Furlong Fitchett, nodding their
heads in unison.
'Heaven, you call it' squeal the mice, 'a fine Heaven
for US . . . we might all be down below, stuck on
toasting forks.'
Well, of course they ARE. That's the Relativity.

*This is a good song to stroke a cat to: I stroke
Lollipop to it.*
*It should be recited hissing all the s's, and rrrolling
all the r's, to represent a cat spitting and purring. It
starts slowly and solemnly (after all, it's a very
serious subject) and gets faster and faster and
faster, with the house and the flat and the view and
the whole, and then a PAUSE before 'Wouldn't be
Parrr-a-dissse'.*

39

FELINE FACT

Cats hunt for sport as much as food
Like Labrador or Setter:
A hungry cat at hunting's good
But a well-fed cat's far better.

*Cats should always be given proper meals at proper
mealtimes: they should NEVER be expected to exist on
the modern paucity of 'rats and mice and such small
deer' as are available for them to catch themselves.*

CHURCHILL AND JOCK

Through total war, in England's finest hour,
He bore the massive gravity of power
That we might live in freedom, always free:

But still the wise Prime Minister found time
To let a friendly sandy kitten climb,
With clumsy kitten-paws, upon his knee.

Ruffling its fur, fondling its ears, once more
He found brief peace within the midst of war.
A time to rest apace and ponder deep

On further strategy, as leader must:
The while his kitten purred in happy trust,
Until it purred itself — and him — to sleep.

To Elder Statesman, in Affairs of State,
The little is as precious as the great.

*Jock was adopted from an R.S.P.C.A. Clinic, as a kitten,
into the home of Sir Winston Churchill. And Churchill was
said to be able to catch a cat-nap at any appropriate
moment, like Napoleon.*

NEMO'S SONG

He's Nobody and Everyone:
Their world revolves around him
Illumined by a brighter sun
Since the halcyon day they found him.

As constant as that guiding star
Brings sailors safe land-view to them
Whoever true cat-lovers are
Their constant cat is true to them.

So Downing Street's brief door may close
Or stormgirt Scillies foam to him:
Wherever Mary Wilson goes
Is always home-sweet-home to him.

*Nemo: the Wilson cat who travels with them, and who
purred so sweetly to her on the B.B.C.*

POLITICAT

Alexander Catullus, please wake up and mew,
The Municipal Elections are practically due:
Tell me, I pray,
That I may
Be correct
And take note — very carefully note —
The best to select:
Tell me, my excellent Cat, for whom will you vote?

Alexander Catullus, asleep on the mat,
Tell me, are you a Conservative Cat?
      'Put out my fish
      In my dish,
      Reach down my cream
      From the shelf — from the top of the shelf —
      Then leave me to dream.
      I am a Cat and the Cat walks by himself.'

Alexander Catullus, asleep on the wall,
Tell me, would you for the Liberal fall?
      ' Wake me up when
      It's mealtime again,
      Skim off the grease
      From the bone — pick the meat off the bone —
      Then leave me in peace.
      I am a Cat and the Cat ponders alone.'

Alexander Catullus, asleep on the cill,
Tell me, would Labour your wishes fulfil?
      'Just brush my fur
      While I purr:
      I'll command, you obey.
      When your work's done — when it's properly done —
      Do please go away.
      I am a Cat and the Cat sleeps in the sun.'

Alexander Catullus, asleep on my lap,
Tell me, are you a Communist mayhap?
    'Don't move your knee:
    Just stroke me.
     Was that TINY share
    Of the turkey-breast – only half of the breast –
    By any means fair?
    I am a Cat and the Cat must get strength to REST.'

ALEXANDER CATULLUS . . . I am ASKING YOUR VIEW. . . .
WHAT Political Party DOES appeal to YOU?
    'Fiddle and fudge
    You're no Judge
    And I'm not
    A defendant – a humble defendant –
    Throw out the lot:
    I'm a Cat and the Cat's Independent.'

LAMENT FOR A LITERARY LADY

'Wake ! for the Golden Cat has put to flight
The Mouse of Darkness with his Paw of Light.'
– OLIVER HERFORD : 'THE RUBAIYAT OF A PERSIAN KITTEN'

PURR MISSIVE   (Puss Puss)

Madam Editor dismisses anything civilised or gentle
as 'too sentimental'
verse
can be interminable or terse,
she'll endorse,
so long as it's coarse
but rhymes
are behind the times
and as for metre and pattern – we've had 'em
says Madam.

poor MADAM is MODERN so MADAM is stuck
with the modern megalomania for multilaterial muck
imagining it
may pass for wit
as graffiti by rude little boys on walls
recalls
we mustn't progress beyond four-letter words
up-to-the-minute herds
have only four fingers, so
inevitably show
that they are too dumb
to count up to five so we have to leave out the thumb.

Poor MADAM is MODERN excuse a laugh
forever
dame clever
too clever by half
claiming LITERATURE must
make a muddy stir
doesn't it just
occur
to her

the wheel keeps turning
full circle spins
the sun still burning
tomorrows sins
twists yesterdays virtues to vice
today
and the CAT has nine lives while the mice
still play.

let monkeys swallow
their putrid potions
ballooning hollow
unkempt emotions
or hippos wallow
in pseudo passions –
the CAT won't follow
slavish fashions.

the CAT climbs high
and the CAT creeps low
so safe walk I
where the CAT may go.

the CAT will deride –
CATS never crawl –
but poor MADAM'S pride
is due for a fall
at long long last
be sure of that
poor MADAM will never get past
the CAT.

UNDRIVEN SNOW
For GEORGE MACBETH from LOLLIPOP

ORLANDO
 Wrote the ORANGE POEM
    Because he is an orange cat

A gorgeous ORANGE POEM
Extensively acclaimed
By ROBERTSON
    Because he also is an orange cat

        He wishes
        He had written it
        Himself

But I
Am a pure
AND HOW PURE
 White Siamese Persian

        Ancestry and Purity
        Are not necessarily synonymous
        And when they mention BASKETS
            They refer
        To what I was brought home in
For I am a pure AND HOW PURE White Siamese Persian

So I
Will write the WHITE POEM

        So WHITE
        Of such IMPECCABLE PERFECTION
            The page
            Will be

            QUITE BLANK

ANY MORE FOR THE SKYLARK LOVER BOY
BEFORE WE SOCK IT TO THEM?

A GOLDEN CAT SONG

For the front-cover portrait of Sir John Smyth's
  'MING'.

Dear is the treasure
Remembrance brings
Of highdays flitten
And faraway things:
Joys that can never
Be bought or sold
Our memories jewels unfold
Their gold.

The pensive pleasure,
One sunlit hour,
Of Burmese kitten
With yellow flower:]
Now and forever
His page shall hold
That golden moment of gold
And gold.

COR LEONIS

NON VINO SED VERITAS
or, more simply, ISS FEY
THE ABSTRACTED ASTROLOGER AND HER CAT

Scene: The Astrologer's Study, decorated in a somewhat Alchemistish manner, with the Signs of the Zodiac and Kabbalistic Emblems much in evidence.

Enter: THE ABSTRACTED ASTROLOGER, a quite delectable young woman, holding a DECANTER which might be imagined to contain the Elixir Vitae or a Love Potion at the very least, but which in fact is about half-filled with Amontillado; followed by her CAT (represented by CHRISTOPHER, an enormous long-haired tabby with white paws and shirtfront).

ASTROLOGER: (*waving her decanter*)	My skies are strewn with flying dragons For all the singing stars that shine Are boundless chains of treasure-wagons Whose jewelled luminence is mine.
CAT: (*very suspiciously*)	Have you assayed that flagon's Wine?
ASTROLOGER: (*paying no heed to such mundane suggestion*)	Should Raphael's maze be Michael's pattern Then Auriel's cube is Gabriel's sphere: My planets spin from Moon to Saturn In nectar flowing crystal clear.
CAT: (*rather gloomily*)	You don't see stars like that on Beer.
ASTROLOGER: (*philosophically*)	No thought's unthought albeit unthinking: When life ends, what shall death begin? What strange celestial circle linking The circuits of the Yang and Yin?
CAT: (*astounded*)	Is this what comes of drinking Gin?

ASTROLOGER :   Who builds with bricks must needs use mortar,
(*well away*)   What rules the heart reveals the brain :
                For me, Llewellyn's Daughter's daughter
                Eternity shall still remain
                    Though I drink soda-water
                    Plain.

The CAT, annoyed at his lines having been taken, stalks out to the kitchen where he discovers that the Astrologer in her Abstraction has forgotten to put away the jug of cream in the refrigerator, and has luckily left it on the table.

It is no longer necessary to put the cream-jug in the refrigerator.

FOUR WHITE KITTENS
A SILENT MIAOW IN HONOUR OF HONOURABLE CAT
For Paul Gallico

Four white kittens
in a pet-shop window –
who will buy them?
will they find good homes?

How can people fond of animals
sentence small kittens to a public window
not knowing who will own them
nor what their fate may be?

They may be lucky:
somebody may buy them
to treat them as cats should be treated –
tenderly cared-for, but cared-for in freedom.
The cat is a free soul
free of mind and free of movement,
above all, free of will.
Not for the cat a dog's abject devotion,
subserviance to a master:
the cat himself is Master,
Lord of the Hearth
and Patron of the Home.

His dignity and grace
his independence
his constant beauty
and his casual kindness,
these are his gifts he gives: if he approves us
the favour he confers by chosen presence
still cannot be commanded.
But tiny kittens innocent and helpless
so vulnerable
before their lion hearts
attain in lion's pride their lion's power –
these four white kittens
in a pet-shop window –
who will buy them?
will they find good homes?

They may be lucky:
but in a pet-shop window
one might be noticed by a foolish woman
who thinks 'it would be nice for little Tommy' –
three years old –
too young to understand
the fragile compass of a living creature:
he'd treat it as a teddy-bear or panda,
to grab it up and throw it down unheeding,
to pester it unceasing for a week
and then discard it,
returning brightly to some other toy.
She means so well –
but let her first imagine
is little Tommy fit to keep a kitten?
Is such a present fair to cat or child?

    Four white kittens
    in a pet-shop window . . .
    who will buy them?
    will they find good homes?

They may be lucky:
But in a pet-shop window
they might be seen by some insensate moron
as fodder for insensate institutions
of conscienceless 'research'.
Insensate 'Scientists' – are they pure sadists?
Or are their brains just blind?
I would subject them to their own equipment
shut them in cages
prod and pry and probe them
to test their nerves un-nerved and to discover
by proof
if they are capable of suffering.

Then when they whined
for mercy and their torment to be ended
I would not answer:
I would re-set the clock for further sessions
and further, further sessions,
keeping them still chained.
I should not speak to them
just raise my eyebrows
and smile
surprised that these insensate subjects
should yet be sensitive themselves
to pain.
How GRATEFUL they should be to be enabled
to show their works results
upon themselves.

But all around the world are many people
who love cats well and wisely:
in shared respect
and common understanding
is perfect company for beast and man
if only each to each may be allied —

> And there are four white kittens
> in a pet-shop window:
> who will buy them?
> They plead so for good homes.

All small creatures are vulnerable: but white kittens more than any other kittens, because they are so very often deaf. A fact which everybody does not know, or realise. A congenitally deaf cat seems to have some compensating, telepathic sense, which makes it a perfect companion. But it does need special consideration. Lollipop is deaf. So was my Paddy Paw.

NEW CAT

Three times this week down Willow Way
I've seen that limping, starveling stray :
I brought her back with me today.

I'll give her what she needs — a home,
Warm shelter from the driving rain —
But Paddy's dish and Paddy's comb
I have no heart to use again.

My porcelain porringers will do
For holding milk and meat for her
And with a *new* comb, brown, not blue.
I'll gently smoothe the tangled fur.

She shall have kindness for his sake :
Her bones, my heart, will cease to ache :
But Paddy's place she cannot take.

*She was by no means to be treated as a second-class
citizen: the new brown comb was more expensive than
the old blue one, and handsome Worcester porringers
were provided as dishes for her daily food.*
*But Paddy's own dish, an Italian pottery one from Harrods,
hand-painted with a cat fishing, remains on the shelf
where it was put away on that desolate sunny Friday
afternoon of September the 9th, 1960.*

ALBUERICUS PAWPINS BEADLE:
PADDY-PAW

The loving, deaf white Persian who was my companion for five happy years: 12th November 1955 to 9th September 1960.

The winter nights are colder
The summer days are bleak:
No longer by my shoulder
His soft paw on my cheek
Will Paddy-Paw be sleeping —
The rosemary evermore
His last long sleep safe-keeping
Must keep my Paddy-Paw.

Rosemary, that's for remembrance: he was buried by the rosemary bush in the garden.

TRYST

Cat, Cat, why do you dance
Before dawn
By the westering moon?

'It will be daybreak soon.
If I dance, there's a chance,
Through the borderline shadows may stir
Thistledown fur –
That shadowless shade
Of the cat who once played
On this lawn –
I am dancing for her.'

*Alexander Catullus, my Lollipop Lexey, dancing in the
very early morning on the lawn where Quillie used to play
with me when I was a child, so many years ago.*

THE KITTENS CAROL

The kings and the shepherds knelt in awe
The cattle stood solemn beside the hay
But a kitten played in the stable straw
And the Sweet Child smiled at the kittens play:

> We wish you well, may your dreams come true:
> This is our Christmas wish for you.
>> (Purr-roo, Purr-roo, Purr-rooo, Purr-roooo.)

They brought gold and frankinscence and myrrh
Those first fore-runners of Santa Claus
But the kitten brought only a blissful purr
And the gentle kneading of velvet paws:

> To wish all well, in a dream come true,
> At Christmastide and all the year through:
>> (Purr-roo, Purr-roo, Purr-rooo, Purr-roooo.)

From that timeless time in the long ago
Linking today with the days far hence
Keep constant the magic of stars and snow
Of Christmas – and kittens – and innocence:

> We wish you well, may your dreams come true:
> This is our Christmas wish for you.
>> (Purr-roo, Purr-roo, Purr-rooo, Purr-roooo).

Written for my Alexander Catullus, Lollipop Lexey, when he was more of a kitten than he is now, at Christmas 1966. It is in the rhythm of his purring, for all kittens everywhere, and all who love cats.

INDEX OF FIRST LINES